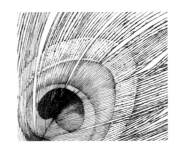

To my parents

A TEMPLAR BOOK
Published in the United States in 1997 by
The Millbrook Press, Inc.
2 Old New Milford Road, Brookfield, CT 06804

Designed and produced by The Templar Company plc
Pippbrook Mill, London Road, Dorking, Surrey RH4 IJE, Great Britain

Copyright © 1997 by The Templar Company plc

Edited by AJ Wood
Designed by Mike Jolley

This book was drawn in ink and painted in watercolor and gouache on watercolor paper.
It was set in 25pt Bernhard Modern.

Library of Congress Cataloging-inPublication Data
Ward, Helen, 1962-
The King of the birds/written and illustrated by Helen Ward.
p.   cm.
Summary: When chaos reigns among the birds, the oldest and wisest
birds declare a contest to determine who will be their king.
ISBN 0-7613-0313-8 (lib. bdg.) ISBN 0-7613-0288-3 (trade)
[1. Folklore.   2. Birds--Folklore.]   I. Title.
PZ8. 1.W2115Ki   1997
398.24'528--dc21   97-2129
CIP
AC

Printed in Belgium

THE
KING *of the* BIRDS

Written & Illustrated by HELEN WARD

THE MILLBROOK PRESS

Brookfield, Connecticut

A long, long time ago, some old
        (but not necessarily wise) birds decided
        that they should have a King. However, they
        could not settle on how or whom to choose.

So messengers were sent out
        to announce a grand gathering...

Big birds...

Small birds...

North birds... South birds...

Up and...

down birds...   Day and night birds.

Here and there birds,

from everywhere... birds were summoned.

Eventually all the birds were gathered together.

The oldest (and possibly wisest) of the old birds called the conference to order and announced their problem...

How do we choose a King?

There was a quietness of deliberation, consideration, and thought. Then came the answers...

"It should be the biggest bird!" said one.

"The smallest bird!" said another.

"The fastest bird!" said a third.

"The fastest runner!"

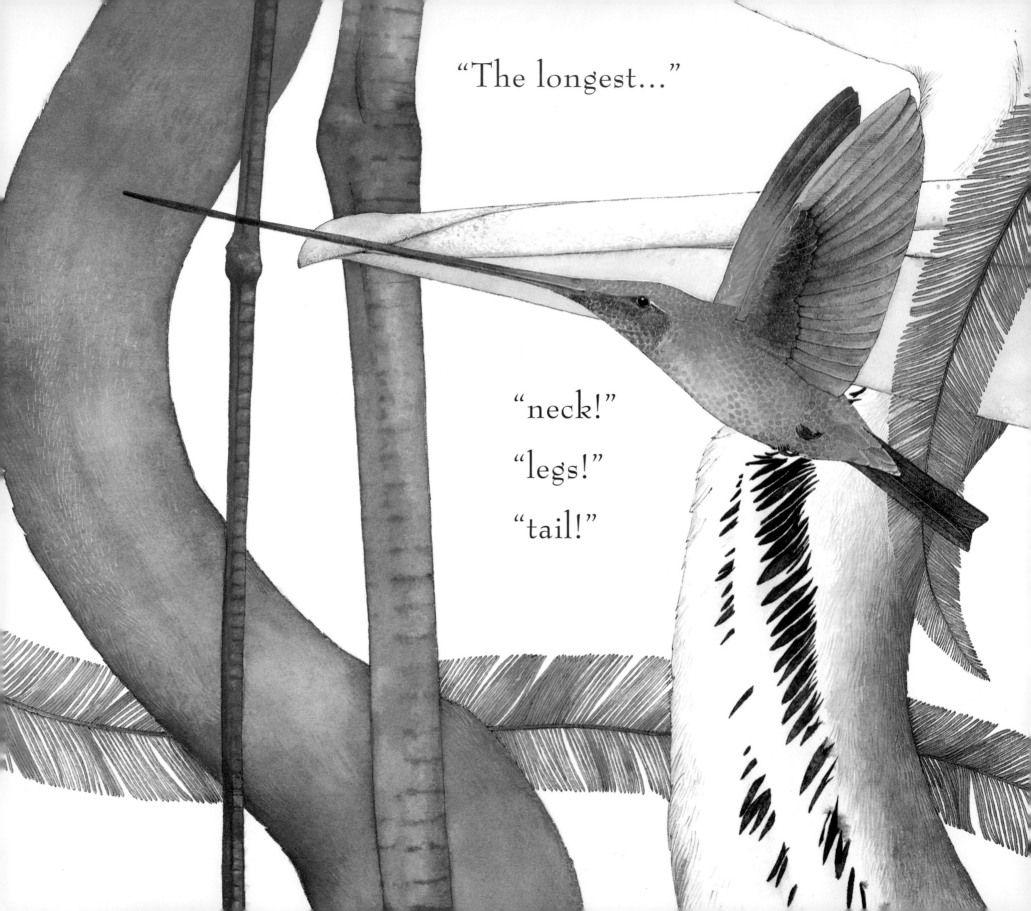

"The longest..."

"neck!"

"legs!"

"tail!"

"The biggest..."

"beak!"

"egg!"

"feet!"

"The most colorful!"

"The most tuneful!"

"The best nest-builder," said the weaverbird.

"The most abundant," said the sparrows.

"The bird with the most spots," said a guineafowl.

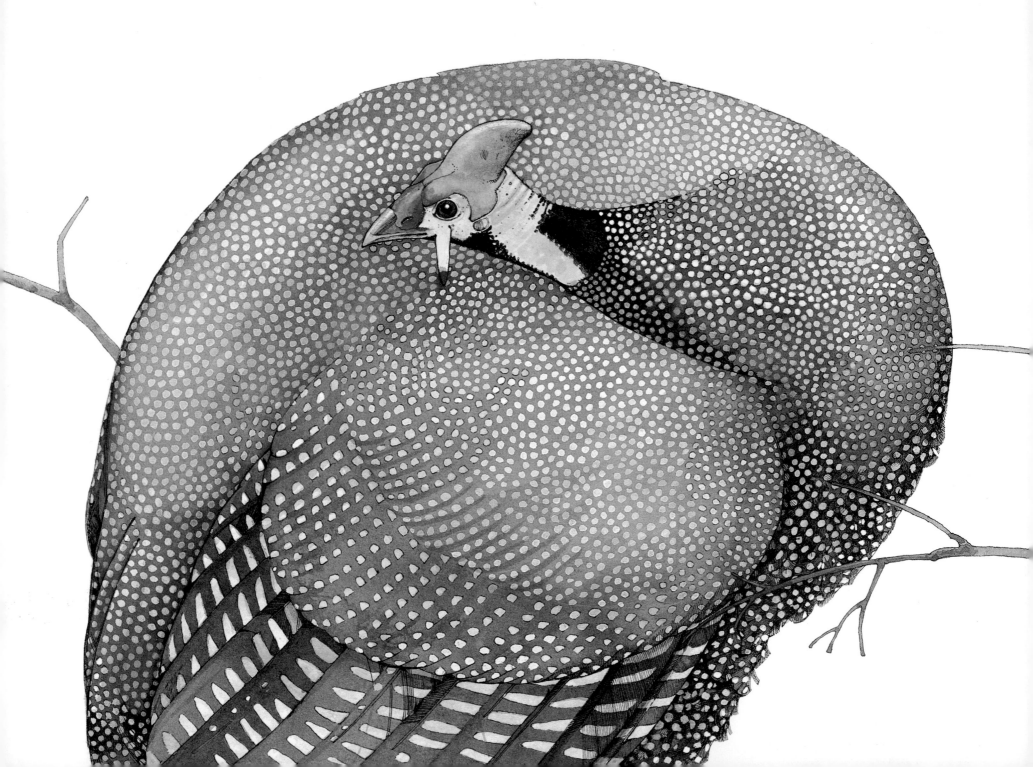

"The bird that looks most like a branch,"
said what looked like a branch.

"Me me me me me!"

said a zebra finch.

Before long there were as many answers as there were birds. And so the birds still had their problem, only now it was bigger, noisier, and more bad-tempered than before.

Finally, after much disgruntled compromising, it was agreed: The bird that could fly the highest would be King.
And because not enough birds could agree on any other plan, the competition began.

All together the birds took to the sky.

They flapped, bounded, leaped and lumbered
into the air like a rising roof of wings...

The struggling broad-bellied birds, the fluttering finches
and sparrows, the lazy flap of the gulls and
slim-winged sea crossers, the busy wings of auks,
and the invisible beats of hummingbirds all rose higher…

and higher, a column of birds
circling up to the sky.

But above them all came the lonely eagle's
patient flap among the wisps of cloud.

"The eagle must be King," said a smaller bird to another. And so a murmur spread slowly through the crowds.

But, just when the eagle could fly no higher...

A wren creeped out of its hiding place
    among the feathers of the eagle's back
    and, beating its little wings furiously,
    it rose into the cold, thin air...
    higher than the eagle...
    higher than all the other birds.

And so it was decided!

The wren and the eagle almost fell back to the ground
where the wren hid hastily in the tangle of a hedge,
safe from the eagle's angry eye.

So the wren became King of the birds.

For, as the oldest (and definitely wisest) birds agreed,

having the highest flier for a King was one thing,

having the cleverest was even better.

THE
KEY *to the* BIRDS

A Long, Long Time Ago... (right)

The gathering of birds includes:

1 & 14. European jay, the messengers

2. Cormorant   3. Emperor penguin

4. Shoebill stork   5. Ibis

6. Turkey   7. Egyptian vulture

8. Wandering albatross   9. Hornbill

10. Marabou stork   11. Raven

12. Grey parrot   13. Owl

Big Birds and Small Birds

Apart from the European jay and the ostrich
(who is, of course, the biggest bird
of all), you will find these small birds (below):

1. Jamaican tody   2. Bee hummingbird

3. Long-tailed tit   4. Red-eared firetail finch

5. Superb fairy wren   6. African pygmy kingfisher

7 & 11. Sunbird   8. Long-tailed manakin

9. Crimson-breasted flower pecker

10. Ruby crowned kinglet

12. Blue tit

North and South Birds

From left to right:

Razorbill; Jackass penguin; Swift; Eiderduck; Skylark;
White-faced scops owl; European jay.

Here and There Birds

Oxpecker and that European jay again!

The Conference

The conference is called to order by a grey parrot -
supposedly one of the world's most intelligent birds.
In the crowd are (right):

1. Iiwi   2. Honeycreeper

3. Sun bittern   4. Pitta

5. Hobby   6. Bullfinch

7. Black grouse   8. Pratincole

9. Flycatcher   10. Red-cheeked cordon-bleu

11. Yellow-headed blackbird 12. Woodpecker

13. Whydah   14. Red-fronted goose

15. Puffbird   16. Java sparrow

17. Trogon   18. Western spinebill

19. King of Saxony bird of paradise

20. White eye

The Fastest Birds

From left to right you can see the roadrunner who can
reach speeds of 26 miles (42kms) per hour, running
across the prairies of North America, and the peregrine
falcon, a wizard on the wing who dives after its prey at
81 miles (131kms) per hour.

The Longest and Biggest

Here are some contestants for the longest and biggest
necks, legs, tails, beaks, feet and eggs. From left to
right: Quetzal (tail), Flamingo (neck), Stilt (leg),
Flamingo (leg), Swordbill hummingbird (beak),
Australian pelican (beak), Goliath heron (neck), Ostrich
(egg), Quail (egg), Bee hummingbird (egg), Jacana
(feet), and Blue-footed booby (feet).

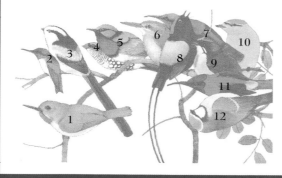

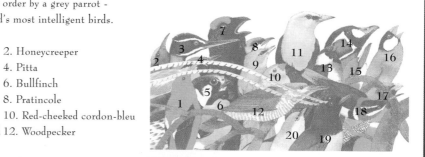

Colorful and Tuneful Birds

Birds are some of the most colorful creatures on Earth. They use color for many things – to attract a mate, frighten their enemies, or help them blend into the background. Above, you can see some colorful specimens:

1. Blue-and-white flycatcher	2. Mandarin duck
3. Maroon-breasted flycatcher	4. Golden pheasant
5. Blue jay	6. Hoopoe
7. Scaled quail	8. Turaco
9. Pitta	10. Crowned crane
11. Violet starling	12. Bullfinch
13. Toucan	14. Swallow tanager
15. Plush capped finch	16. Gouldian finch
17. Fairy bluebird	18. Tragopan
19. Cuckoo roller	20. Parakeet
21. Blue crowned pigeon	22. Green magpie
23. Swallow tailed gull	24. Sunbird
25. Bee eater	26. Puffin
27. Superb fruit dove	28. Cardinal

The most tuneful bird is, of course, the nightingale.

The Best Nest...

Birds build many different kinds of nests. You can see three of them here. From left to right: Weaverbirds build upside-down nests of grass with the entrance at the bottom; Tailorbirds weave together leaves; and Oropendulas make huge baggy nests that hang from the branches of trees. The most common bird in the world is the English, or common sparrow – and it really is common! You can find it in almost every single country on Earth.

Spotty Specimens

From left to right you can see:

Spotted guineafowl - these birds are related to turkeys. Their spotted feathers help to camouflage them against their backgrounds, protecting them from would-be predators. They are found throughout Africa though you are more likely to see their domesticated descendants scratching around in the farmyard. Tawny frogmouth - this nocturnal insect hunter spends its day resting in a tree where its mottled plumage blends perfectly with the bark on which it sits. If danger threatens it will point its head skywards in imitation of a dead branch. It uses the same technique at dusk to prey on passing insects, frogs and snails. It lives in Australia. Zebra finch - A common cage bird, this finch can be found throughout Australia where it lives in large flocks.

A Quarrelsome Crowd (above)

1. Peacock	2. Chaffinch
3. Waxwing	4. Starling
5. Caique	6. Fieldfare
7. Peking robin	8. Blue jay
9. White-bellied plumed pigeon	

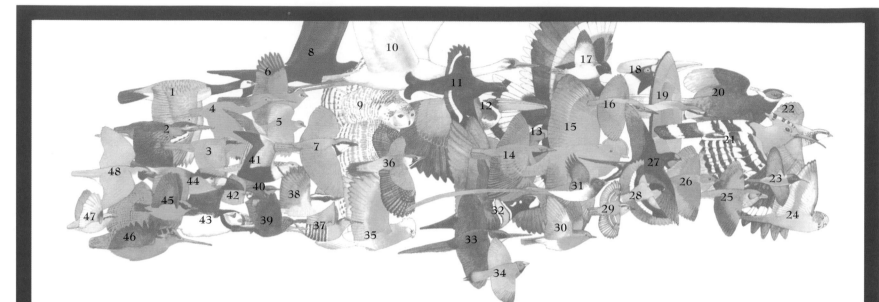

The Competition Begins

A huge array in an aerial display (above)!

1. Barnacle goose
2. Green heron
3. Mot-mot
4. Scarlet ibis
5. Orange dove
6. Turaco
7. Bulbul
8. Frigate bird
9. Snowy owl
10. Crane
11. Black grouse
12. Pelican
13. Purple swamp hen
14. Cotinga
15. Cock-of-the-rock
16. Kingfisher
17. Auk
18. Hornbill
19. Bee eater
20. Brown-eared pheasant
21. Hoopoe
22. Partridge
23. Sunbird
24. Budgerigar
25. Barbet
26. Bluebird
27. Swallow
28. Bullfinch
29. Goldcrest
30. European robin
31. Paradise flycatcher
32. Harlequin duck
33. Paradise jacamar
34. Gouldian finch
35. Galah
36. Woodpecker
37. Rail
38. Kiskadee
39. Silktail
40. Varied thrush
41. Black-bellied sandgrouse
42. Painted quail
43. Puffin
44. Laminated-bill toucan
45. Vermillion flycatcher
46. American woodcock
47. Nuthatch
48. Woodswallow

Those That Were Left

There are many flightless birds in the world, from fast-running ostriches to penguins who cannot fly but are experts in the water. Here you can see, from left to right, the kiwi, an extraordinary "furry" looking bird found only in New Zealand, and the Okinawa rail from Japan.

Up in the Air (below)

1. Spoonbill
2. Booby
3. Condor
4. Wandering albatross
5. Flamingo
6. Frigate bird
7. Goose
8. Pelican
9. Stork
10. Ibis
11. Ruddy turnstone
12. Arctic tern
13. Golden eagle

And When the Eagle Could Fly No Higher...

A fine array of beaks, from left to right:
Gannet; Bee eater; Scarlet ibis; Californian quail; Loon; Little plover; Toucan; Black skimmer; Woodcock; Andean cock-of-the-rock; Cormorant; Oxpecker; Kookaburra; Barbet; Spoonbill; Anhinga.

And Most Important of All...

Golden eagle - there are many types of eagles but the golden is one of the best known and most numerous in the world. It can fly at speeds of nearly 80 miles (125 kms) an hour as it soars the skies in search of its prey. It also performs spectacular flight displays, swooping and curling through the air in a demonstration of its aerial accomplishments. Wren - by contrast, the tiny wren is more usually found scuttling around in undergrowth where it is often mistaken for a small mammal. It is an excellent and varied songster and is crafty enough to make dummy nests to divert potential predators away from its real nest site – hence its reputation for being clever!